NO CAPE *Necessary*

NO CAPE *Necessary*

Saving yourself from destructive patterns
and finding your inner Superhero

DANI ATKINS

Charleston, SC
www.PalmettoPublishing.com

No Cape Necessary

First Edition

Hardcover ISBN: 978-1-68515-037-2
Paperback ISBN: 978-1-68515-038-9
eBook ISBN: 978-1-68515-039-6

Table of Contents

Introduction

They say that it only takes ten to fifteen seconds of smiling to trick your brain into thinking you're happy.

Isn't that crazy?

And when experiencing something traumatic, we're encouraged to take full, slow, deep breaths to calm down. We aren't actually close to calming down at that moment and often resent the person helping us count ("In one, two, three, four, out one, two, three, four"), but gradually, focusing on decreasing the panicked adrenaline rush by mindful breathing tricks our mind into believing we are calm. So if we can engage in an activity to switch an emotion from grumpy to glad, from anxious to calm, surely there is a set of activities that could help us switch our mindsets from an undesirable place to a positively empowered one. And that's what this journey is all about.

We each face great defeats at some point in our lives—loss of loved ones, loss of jobs, loss of relationships, loss of individuality—and often we accept those defeats and losses while slapping a label onto our skin: victim. Once that label's been placed, it's hard to peel off. It's like one of those sticker price tags stuck on the bottom of a new coffee mug—nearly impossible to remove in one piece. We read books on how to recover from codependency, we listen to confidence-building and strategy-building podcasts, we journal a thousand pages of heart-wrenching prose, but somehow, we still feel stuck in our personal victimhood.

So let's be effectively proactive and get rid of it once and for all, shall we? In this book, we're diving in and discovering actions to help "trick" our mind into releasing the label "victim" and replacing it with a new, empowered one: hero. We're going to freakin' save ourselves from victimhood and rise into a new positively charged mindset that will allow us to become fully who we'd love to be! And if you want to see that happen in your life, by all means, let's go for a ride! I am delighted to share with you what I discovered to be effective to get me out of the deep, dark chasm of victimhood and rise to a confidence level I hadn't experienced ever before.

You see, before this shift occurred in my life, I was the most brokenhearted, self-labeled loser. I needed to *do* something to get myself out of the misery of my post-toxic-relationship state. I was grappling with understanding who I really was after years of not-so-confidence-building messaging from my significant other, and cords of insecurity kept me captive in that confused state of mind even months after the breakup. Even with thirteen years of experience empowering adults through teaching dance and a season of life coach certification training, I couldn't get out of my emotional rut. I couldn't shake my self-inflicted victimhood. That is, not until this idea came to life and took form as the "Eight-Week Superhero Challenge." Developing it as a self-saving strategy and experimenting with it on myself, I realized quickly how potent the concepts were and how effective the changes became through time.

And this is why I am thrilled to share this insight with you! Not only did it make for the best summer in my life, but I am still reaping the benefits of the challenge years afterward. The adventures I've experienced, the friendships I've built, the love I have found, and the powerful me I have discovered since this journey are things I wish everyone to find for themselves!

So let's go on this journey together. Get ready—you're not just reading about these things but exercising them yourself! Find a journal to write down what you discover. Even if you don't feel like you have tons of enthusiasm for writing, just follow along as best as you can. Make the decision that you are going to get your "powers" back and discover some new ones along the way. Because you are reading this, you are telling yourself you are ready. So here we go! Up, up, and away!

Origin Story

You arouse from a deep slumber.

At least you think you've awoken. It's hard to tell if you're truly awake or still asleep when you can't see a thing around you. You hold your hand before you and can barely make out the shadowy outlines of your fingers. Pebbles press into your hand as you push yourself to sit—how on earth did you get here? You feel the space around you: the gravel floor, the cool cement wall beside you, the old smell of cold, damp air hanging thick about you. Echoes reverberate through the chamber with every scuff of movement you make.

Slowly rising from the ground, you try to soften your movements although your heartbeat pounds in your ears. Who else is here? Maybe whoever brought you to this place? Or maybe another lost soul? But no—you can feel it in the silence; you are alone.

You are unshackled and, in many ways, *free*. But why can't you shake the feeling that you are still completely at the mercy of the villain who put you away? Because surely someone put you there—you have no recollection of taking a nice, long, meandering stroll deep into God knows where. You are grappling with defeat and shame—how on earth did they get you here? You feel small. Unnoticed. Lost.

This is victimhood. This is post-abuse. This is the aftermath of infuriating circumstances. This is the moment when hopes are dashed and it's hard to see what could possibly come next that would bring us to a new frame of mind and living. This is the story many of us are living right now. This state of things seems dismal, trying, and hopeless. But this is where we *start* our journey and where we begin to grow—from the darkness.

Although it's a familiar origin story to many, we often forget that that's just what it is—an origin story, not the entire saga.

I like to think of this chasm being like the one a young man named Bruce fell down before finding himself amid a swarm of bats that, while probably terrifying him to no end, also revved up a passion for vengeance in his heart and unleashed a drive to become a mighty superhero who would bring justice to criminals throughout his hometown. He tumbled down that space after witnessing something very traumatic, and the tumble down the bat-hole just added to the trauma.

Anyway, this dark space, this metaphor of the grief we experience after something beyond our control happens to us, is somewhere many of us stay for quite a while. Imagine Bruce deciding to stay in there with all those bats, maybe feeling a tinge of inspiration, maybe deciding to wait it out because he liked feeling hopeless (since, you know, it takes much more energy to hope and act on hope than it does to feel hopeless). I wonder what would have happened to his home city. I wonder what would have happened to his family's legacy. I wonder what would've happened to *him*.

Once upon a time, I stumbled into a chasm myself. I was fresh out of a toxic relationship and felt myself still being used by my ex, so I blindly ran myself into that chasm of victimhood and stayed there, hanging out with the bats, fallen and miserable. And there, I was captive in that metaphorical dark chasm of misery, of bleakness, of self-doubt and hate. And I did the thing I'm thankful Bruce didn't do but I'm sad that I did: I stayed there because I liked feeling hopeless. I didn't have to feel accountable if I felt hopeless. There were moments in that broken-off relationship when I was truly overpowered and couldn't do anything in that moment. But even after falling into that chasm, clearing my head a little, and shaking off the dirt, I still stayed down there, waiting to be saved by someone else. Just waiting. I think it's easy for us to get trapped inside those thoughts. The negative thoughts are such a spiral down the drain, and we just circle round and round in this whirlpool with no real way out except to go further and further down into the dark mire of our negative beliefs. It's uncomfortable down there, but it feels safe and predictable.

My aha, emerging-from-the-bat-cave moment came to me in a phone conversation with my mother regarding "Oh, woe is me! I feel betrayed and double-crossed and stupid" and yada, yada, yada. And then came the bat. It flew in the form of words from my mom: "You just need to find a nice Christian boy to marry and settle down with."

Her words hit me like she had just told me to go to hell, because that's what I realized I would be doing if I followed her advice at that moment. Not because it was the worst advice, but because that was the very *last* thing I needed. And I let her know, vehemently:

"Really? *Really*?! I need a *man* to help me fix the problems caused by *a man*? Really? Do you know who I would attract now in this vulnerable state, Mother? *The exact same type of man who put me here!* A man who sees himself as a knight in shining armor! And you know what happens when this type of guy stops feeling like your savior? He pushes you right back down into the dirt in some sick way just so he can feel like he's saving you again! *And* he'll somehow manipulate you to believe that it didn't ever happen and that you're crazy for thinking he's ever been anything but gallant to you, even if he's punched you or spit at you or AGGGGHHH! No, if I need anything, I need to save myself. I need to...save...myself."

And there. That moment of rage turned into a moment of clarity. I sat down slowly, excusing myself and hanging up the phone, soaking in the words and the idea that had just come to me in a flash. The summer sun streamed through my window, dust particles floating through the roasting-hot living room. It was almost like each speck of dust was an idea, floating around me, urging me to pay attention to them as they danced before me. That aha moment still strikes me as one of the strongest I've ever had in my life, not for the rudimentary ideas that were just taking form, but for the results those ideas would bring forth in my life.

I had been thrashing around in pain as a victim, but my severe emotional wounds needed healing, not thrashing. And if I wanted help but knew I was in such a fragile state that I couldn't trust the people who would show up, eager and desperate to help, then I needed to do it myself. I needed to save myself, to become my own damn knight in shining armor. I had to change. I had to encourage myself to change instead of berating myself for my mistakes—and maybe that's where the primary source of my victimizing came from: *me* constantly reliving the abuse and punishing myself over and over again like it was actually going to teach me a lesson.

All of my reasons to stay in the chasm were valid, as I definitely needed a haven for healing at one point, but I realized I was clinging to my victimhood a little too proudly and didn't need that anymore. The chasm had served its purpose, and now it was time for me to fulfill mine.

This is a difficult conclusion. On one hand, it's exciting to know you have a different vision of your future than just sitting around, binge-watching your favorite sitcom for the umpteenth time, distracting yourself with the different crunching sounds that come from various brands of potato chips, and hiding away from society. On the other hand, how does one simply break through years of certain habits, reactions, and thought processes? Oh, and trauma? Change is hard! But I knew in my heart of hearts that I wanted a different role because I didn't want people to feel sorry for me; I wanted people to be *inspired* by me.

In any "spider bite," "bats of inspiration," aha moment, there will be growing pains. But the great news is that we are designed to adapt to change! Our teeth come in when we're infants and developing the ability to digest solid foods to chew, they fall out and larger ones grow in as we evolve into our more developed preteen selves, and again they fall out as our body grows tired and processes nutrients differently to sustain us for the remainder of our lives. And that's a long process of just our teeth! Don't even get me started on the speedy replacement of every cell in our body. But these are physical reminders that we are designed to grow and evolve and change. Our mind is designed to change too. We have chemicals in our brain that encourage different types of thoughts and energies to ebb and flow and adapt to our environment. Sometimes they can be a little haywire, but that's why we learn techniques to help us sort out true feelings from ego.

Let's say you relate thoroughly to being trapped in a chasm. Been there, done that, kinda tired of it, and want a new place to hang out. Let's first begin by making a different choice. Your mind is full of chatter from every perspective your mind can dream up, so let's listen to the ones that say you have a special role on the planet. Do you hear that one? Let's lean into that voice's direction because that statement is true: you do have a special role. Your picking up and reading this book is a testament to your belief that somehow that's true. So yay! You just tied a belief to an action—the best way to build a new truth!

If you've seen the marvelous animated film *Frozen II*, it's a beautiful illustration of a voice that calls to us, showing us truth, guiding us to greatness, and taking us on an incredible journey. That's us and our lives! You could burrow into our personal chasms of misery and shame, claiming the role of victim, but you are designed to be an interesting, engaging protagonist that a voice of great destiny calls to! You could lash out and throw your pain onto others, claiming the role of villain (because, let's face it, we have *all* done some version of that at some point), but we all have a desire deep down inside of us to bring good to the world and be a hero to our loved ones and community.

All of this to say, *you* choose your character's role. You're given a body to work with, a unique personality, a unique origin story, a special and interesting plot—you have all the makings of an amazing protagonist! Christopher Reeve once said that a hero is "an ordinary individual who finds the strength to persevere and endure in spite of overwhelming obstacles." Are you ready to really dive into what that could mean for you? Are you ready to discover how epic your life could be? Are you willing to do what it takes to fulfill a thrilling destiny?

I believe you are.

I believe in you.

Now grab your metaphorical cape—we've got some saving to do!

* * *

RECAP:

This is the part of the chapter where I will ask you thought-provoking questions, and you can choose to journal or just think through your answers.

Also, in future chapters, this is where you will find fun activities listed to activate the concepts and traits within each section. So definitely don't miss out on this part! This part is all about you, babe!

Week 1: Strategy

I felt the dramatic pull of my heart to do something once the notion struck me while on the phone with my mother. I looked around my tiny living room with about ten self-help books scattered around the coffee table and couch, wondering what the hell I'd been doing about any of those pages and pages of wisdom I'd studied month after month. I had dived into so many books on mindset and positivity; I had watched every TED Talk imaginable on every relevant topic; I had immersed my brain in the words and ideas of others, hoping something would rub off, determined to conjure my newly improved self through study, meditation, and drowning out the voices of doubt in my mind.

All of this inspiration started fluttering around in my head like pieces of paper ripped up into tiny pieces of confetti—present and accounted for but jumbled and floating, detached from their significant meaning. I concluded at that point, with this much information, I had to change my process in order for any of it to make a difference. I had to let my actions speak louder than my words. My brain understood the knowledge to an extent, but up until it was an active part of my life, it would remain dormant and cooped up, like a chick waiting to hatch from its egg without pecking or kicking the shell.

Among the pile of books upon my coffee table, I found a journal, the journal that had logged my pain and victim mentality for over a season. Now it was going to experience a new narrative. If books could talk, I mused, this one was going to say something like "Um, Dani, is that still you? Wow, did you lose weight? Like the weight of a thousand pounds of shame and despair? Yeah? Wow! Good job!"

But how did I want to start? Where did I begin? With all the desire and ideas and feelings tumbling around like a dryer on high, I was beginning to feel overwhelmed. Again. I needed to simplify, but what did I need to simplify? I got real comfy on my couch, pen and journal in hand, and simply, stream of consciousness style, wrote everything down.

Save myself. Become my own hero. Acquire superpowers (hah!). Hero. What is a hero? What would it take to become one? If I need to prove to myself that I'm in a different role than the one I've practiced for God knows how long, what do I need to do? And how long is it going to take? What could I practice? Actions speak louder than words. What actions? In his book *Atomic Habits*, James Clear says, "Every action you take is a vote for the person you want to become." So what was the first step in emotionally registering to vote?

Little did I know that my little brainstorm writing sesh was the first key element in my journey to come. Every traveler needs a roadmap (or GPS). So I knew my destination: hero. And this writing session was the calibrating and planning I needed to get there.

Because, my friends, every great intention needs a great *strategy* to support it.

The time to develop a strategy is one of the most important things in personal growth. Most people that the world would deem "successful" wake up in the morning and give themselves a full hour to themselves (maybe two!) to set their intentions, meditate, clear their mind, and prep themselves for the day ahead of them with a clean slate. So I decided to take that entire afternoon, one of the few free blocks of time I had that entire summer, to clarify exactly what I wanted out of this idea, this journey, this experiment.

So let's go on this brainstorming train together, shall we?

First: what does it mean to be a hero?

I decided the best way to address this was to figure out *who* were my heroes. Fiction, nonfiction, friends, family—who did I see as heroic in my life? Were they fast, strong, healing, young, old, common, epic? I searched my imagination for who had inspired me in the past, recalling the days as a child when I would watch the old TV show *Zorro* in black and white at my grandparents' house. I thought of my very favorite literary character, Sydney Carton, whose heroism inspired me to compose a soundtrack for *A Tale of Two Cities* when I was in high school. I thought of my aunt Ginger, a previous cancer survivor, who had passed away from a third or fourth bout of it when I was sixteen years old. I thought about Martin Luther King Jr. and the momentum he generated in social justice and equality. I wrote down anything that jumped to mind that lit a spark of inspiration.

Scribbling furiously, I urgently filled two pages of my journal to the margins and then sighed in relief. I was done. I sat back and looked at the list I had before me, thankful for all of these characters and humans who gave me such a clear picture of who I would like to be, to all the authors and creators who had a mind of what was admirable, and to the comic book genre for such exaggerated forms of these types of extraordinary humans.

So here is a moment for *you* to think about who *you* admire most and consider heroic. Don't even think about why—some of the characters and people who come to mind might not make a bit of sense. If you have a pen and paper nearby, grab them. Write down these people that jump into your mind. If they all fall into one genre, try to think of another branch of inspiration you admire as well. For instance, if you can only think of historical figures, think about the people you admire in your personal life, movies that you've seen, TV and YouTube personalities, characters from novels or manga or comic books…There are so many sources of inspiration in this journey! Do this exercise for ten minutes. You'll find it easy for the first minute or two and then you'll draw a blank, but keep at it and go with your gut—you might be surprised which people or even animals spark energy in your mind.

After I wrote down my heroes, I began to process the *why*. I know there's a whole theory to start with *why*, but in this instance it was easiest for me to start with *who*. I assessed my list. I appreciated the diversity of types of humans because that made the *why* clear to be seen. So I then decided to look at the common threads. Superheroes, Sydney Carton, Aunt Ginger, Mulan…What did they all have in common?

I began list two: the common qualities list. I found a lot of bravery, which meant they had to overcome fear; they fought for innocent lives, or they demonstrated great physical and mental strength to push through a challenge, they all knew how to move people with their words, and so on. It looked like a connect-the-dots puzzle or a conspiracy theorist's scribbling as I was drawing lines and arrows across the pages in black and red ink and the occasional green highlight (since green is my personal power color).

Quick! If you wrote down your heroes, look at it! What are the commonalities you see between them? What do you value most about the "superteam" of favorite characters you just constructed? Are their stories and journeys similar to yours? Do they beat up bad guys? If so, why? What type of villains do they face? Do they love pizza as much as you do? Do they have spiffy cars? Write down the traits you see many of them have in common.

I tallied up and found twelve qualities that seemed to run true from character to character. Then I wrote out list three: What action could go with each quality? How could these traits take physical form in the most immediate ways possible to exercise? This stumped me a little as I analyzed each word written within that list. What could I physically do to announce to myself and to the universe that "I'm taking on this new role now and forevermore, so *hah*! So long, sucker!" (I would say this while kicking the door closed on my victimhood). If I found a quality that I couldn't think up a physical action I could connect to it, I would see if I could pair the intention with a similar quality that did have an action. For instance, I blended wisdom with communication, compassion with sacrifice, and so on.

That's when this whole thing started becoming an actual, physical challenge. It started taking on a name. It started looking recognizable. Then came the conundrum: how long was this challenge going to take? Three months? Four weeks? Seven days? A year? In Jewish and Christian spiritual writings, it's common to see the number forty as a timeframe for growth or gestation: it rained forty days and forty nights and the world flooded during Noah's time, the Israelites wandered the desert for forty years, Jesus spent forty days in the wildness being tempted by Satan…

In any case, I decided that my challenge would be eight weeks since forty weekdays sounded like a perfect timeframe to work with. Ya know, no big deal or anything. Just eight weeks to change my life. That's all.

I felt extremely empowered as I pored over my notes, my road map to my new role. After consolidating my qualities list, I had eight to practice. Eight heroic traits in eight weeks. And that was the official birth of the Eight-Week Hero Challenge.

Since I was already organizing it and creating an epic strategy to fulfill my mission, that first day marked the first phase of "strategy week." I was going to hammer in my intention, lock in commitments to fulfill my desire of saving myself, and share with my best friends what I was doing so I would be accountable to them for my progress. Strategy was such a crucial part of all of my heroes' story arcs. No one accidentally lives a consistently epic life. No one accidentally consistently does great good in the world.

In 2002, the Oakland A's came into the baseball season as one of the worst teams in the league with a history of failure. They had a shitty budget and therefore couldn't acquire the highly sought-after players with amazing stats the other teams could draft. Things were looking bleak until the team manager got some insight and advice from a statistics specialist. Together, they were able to see patterns of the players they did have on the team, notice some undervalued traits of the players that were there, recognize that the few standout players on their team really didn't add enough value when it came to the small tasks that, when push came to shove, made a huge difference in the game, and they were able to make a few good trades for players that fit specific tasks and roles they needed filled on their roster. Now, it didn't happen overnight, but by gradually weighing the skills and making shifts in their batting lineup and game strategies, they managed the incredible feat of winning twenty games in a row! It's easy to understand how that's a pretty big deal, especially coming from the lowest ranking team in the league, but guess when that had happened last? Not since 1935! In other words, it's ridiculously rare, even for the best teams in baseball! And this was all due to meticulous strategic planning.

Returning to *you* and *your* goals, *your* heroes, and *your* qualities, what do you see shouting at you from the pages of your journal? Are you seeing your core values sing out? Maybe they've been hiding for a spell because they weren't allowed to shine or share their voice in the toxicity of your past circumstances or in the depths of the chasm, but are you seeing them now? Find the qualities that really jump out at you, that make your skin hum, that make your heart jump in excitement.

In order to really get things organized and going for yourself during this phase, here's what to do:

Start with mindset. Wake up thinking, *Today is going to be awesome.* Say it out loud! Tell yourself "Today is going to be awesome" with every step to the bathroom or the living room or wherever your first steps of the morning take you.

When you get to wherever that place is, say to yourself, "Today is already awesome, and it's only just begun!" Say it over and over, and this time, smile! If you've said it ten times and you still don't really feel it, say it ten more times. Do you feel it? Can you picture the beautiful day ahead of you?

Look in the mirror and say, "I can't wait to see what the day will bring me! I receive it with open arms!" Open your palms and reach out like you're about to receive a present. Repeat this ten times.

Again, if you aren't really vibing with the phrase, try saying it ten more times or reword it to something that feels empowering to you, and then move on to your last mini-mantra: "I feel awesome, I look awesome, I kick ass, and I can't wait to meet the version of myself on the other side of this hero challenge." Do this in front of the mirror and *make eye contact*. Like the awkward kind of eye contact you wouldn't really make with anyone else (except for maybe your best friend when you're messing around and purposely making them uncomfortable for a laugh). Say the phrase in a hushed tone, a normal tone, and a commanding tone. Say it like you're practicing a script for your dream role in a movie. Say it like you're preparing for battle. Say it, feel it, and if you're not feeling it, breathe and visualize what that looks like. Picture yourself high-fiving people at a food drive or seeing your ex and not even recognizing them because the trigger no longer exists. Picture yourself giving a speech, your audience rapt with attention, roaring with applause with your conclusion. Picture yourself living in confidence, where you can go anywhere and feel you belong, have value, make a big difference, and that your place in the world matters.

Because, by the way, it *does*. And that's what this challenge is all about. But every morning during this week of strategy, part of your process is *amping yourself up* to the point where you kick off the covers immediately in response to your alarm and shout, "Let's *do this*!" and then say your mantras with that same enthusiasm as you start your day.

Warning: if you have never said mantras out loud before, it may feel a little silly at first. Especially if you have a nosy or judgy roommate. But, if need be, play some music to drown it out to everyone but yourself. Because your strategy week is helping you set the feeling for the rest of the week and, essentially, the challenge.

Your mind, body, and soul all need to be activated in conjunction to take this journey because it will affect *everything*. In amazing ways, you'll find shifts in places that you didn't even realize had shifting to do!

Additionally, and this is very important, use this week to share the deets with people who care about you most and will cheer you on! If that means you only tell one person you're about to embark on an epic emotional journey, that's great! If they respond with "I have no idea what the hell that means, but let me know how it goes! It sounds intriguing!" keep them in the loop. If they respond with "What the hell…? You just made it weird," don't worry about it. There are other people who will be more than thrilled to cheer you on. I will, for instance! I'm totally there with you all the way!

The point is to find someone who is interested enough in your growth that you can update them randomly if something fun happens or if you need a buddy to bounce an idea off or something. Post on social media if you really want to make a statement like "Hello, world! I'm kicking ass and taking names because I am on a hero's journey!" Accountability is *key* when it comes to growth. We can only do so much when left to our own devices.

Oh, and by the way, while you make the calls and texts to your potential cheerleaders, make sure you reach out to the places and people that could be instrumental in helping you achieve your herodom in the next eight weeks—volunteer centers, photographer for your kick-ass boudoir hero photoshoot, rock climbing partners, violin teacher…you get the picture. One of the main elements in any epic saga is that there is a guide/sage/helper of sorts who assists the hero in accomplishing their end goal, so we're going to exercise this element of the story formula and find our helpers and guides to make our epic experience the best it possibly can be.

Now that we have locked it in with our guides and helpers, we have to lock it in with ourselves, and that means looking at your schedule for the next eight weeks and seeing where a big action can take place every week. It means committing to some type of journaling daily, even just a quick jot before bed. You will want to document your progress over these next eight weeks because, trust me, someday you'll want to look back and review all the things that happened to make such an impact on your life, and it will be nice to have the documentation to report those things.

Oh, and I do have one additional thing to remind you in your planning time: remember that this growth is *fun*. And it's supposed to be *fun*.

Yes, it packs a wallop to our self-doubt and pity, which might feel a little foreign and unsettling at times, but it is supposed to be and is designed to be *fun*. Why? Because as you're going through the motions, you're going to need to allow yourself to feel some positive feelings. Especially if you're used to living your life in low vibration zones. There may be some days or some challenges that feel more difficult than others, some less delightful, maybe, but remember that there is joy in running toward the light! Every sliver of sunlight you see in that chasm will spark hope that soon you will feel the warmth and light of day!

So there you have it.

The gauntlet has been thrown down. Are you ready for the challenge? Are you ready for your first week of your hero's journey? Well, ready or not, here it comes!

* * *

RECAP:

Within this chapter, we talked about brainstorming to find your personal epic heroes, qualities, and actions. To follow along with the themes I chose, you can plan your challenge similarly. The weeks are as follows:

Week 1: Strategy=planning it all out and locking it in

Week 2: Learn to Fight=take self-defense

Week 3: Facing Fears=create and share something honest and vulnerable

Week 4: Sacrifice and Compassion=give up coffee, give donations, forgiveness practices

Week 5: Battle Cry=start a blog, speak up

Week 6: Adventure=do something new, go somewhere new

Week 7: Superteam=celebrate amazing people

Week 8: Learn to Fly=the big grand gesture to yourself

To customize your Eight-Week Hero Challenge experience, immerse yourself in meditations, books, and actions that embody your chosen theme(s) each week. Read on to see how I implemented my action steps and where I found inspiration, so that you can use this as a guide for your own journey.

Week 2: Learn to Fight

I stared at him across the mat.

"Really?" I asked hesitatingly.

"Yes." He nodded, settling into a wide stance only a yard away from me. He was a stranger to me, but he was the professional. Who was I to argue with his methods? He reached a hand toward my throat. What a trigger! I'd had a hand there before and had felt so helpless, so my recalled panic rushed in like a wave, flipping into indignance, and I reacted with a snarl. My hands found their grip on his shoulders, one at a time, as I thought, *Knee,* right hand, *of,* left hand, *VENGEANCE*! My knee flew up, full speed, and made contact up between his open legs.

When was the last time you watched a movie about a hero that didn't have some type of fight scene in it? Even if you think, "Oh, I totally did about that fireman one time who saved a cat after saving a kid and his grandma and after he snapped his femur," think again! There's a fight in there too. Maybe not against the traditional villain, but there's definitely a force they needed to combat.

It is in our nature to fight. To push back. To survive.

We have chemicals in our brain that release adrenaline and give us the urge to punch and kick and bite or to run away. Throughout time, we have been tuned in to sense the environment around us, and if it was safe, cool! Let's sit and eat something. If not, pick up the biggest rock you can and hurl it at that shadow moving in the corner! Oh no! It's right behind you! *Ruuunnn!*

Our instinct to fight served us very well back in the day in those eat-or-be-eaten environments. In our modern world, however, it makes life stressful for seemingly no reason. We sit at our desk and, out of the blue, we sense someone is going to take credit for our work and, oh no! That survival instinct just kicked in, and now we are boiling hot with rage, steam blowing from our ears. How the hell *dare they*. Never mind there is no real evidence to support it other than a stray comment by the water cooler regarding someone noticing the project we're working on and remarking on how it's the super coolest and how they wish they had come up with the idea. And our brain starts screaming *Danger, Will Robinson, danger* over and over again, making it hard to get back to the project at hand or, really, think about anything else. Our fight-mode button has been pushed because, in a strange, roundabout way, we're feeling our survival threatened.

And you're starting to see this type of rage as fairly normal. Who hasn't seen the thousands of "Karen" videos flying throughout the interwebs being shared because it's hard to believe that people can flip out over such trivial things. That, however, doesn't put the rest of us in the clear. Smearing others and putting them down is like fighting dirty, and wow, is that prevalent and actually socially acceptable in many ways. Threatening to fight is kinda like throwing the first punch. Like when you write a terrible Yelp review because your waiter brought your food a moment later than you had wished. Never mind they were understaffed—they didn't give you immediate service, so you had to fight back somehow.

Yes, there are so many thoughtless ways we go into fight mode, but there are many amazing ways to vent our rage and aggression and, amazingly, not hurt people. I mean, it sounds like a win-win, and it's strange that we're not all massively training ourselves every day in all of these alternate ways that, I believe, are our next stage of evolution. But, of course, I know I'm tremendously at fault in improperly venting my fight-or-flight impulses, so who am I to judge?

Which is why I determined the second week in my Eight-Week Superhero Challenge would be to address my rage, figure out which fear it stemmed from, and find a way to channel it. There are so many great practices to fight and tame the rage monster, methods like working out, meditation and deep breathing, writing in a journal, energy-releasing mantras, hakas, martial arts, and others. And since many of my heroes were warriors, it only made sense to channel fighting my rage monster into learning to actually fight responsibly. In hindsight, I couldn't have picked a better activity because:

1. I wanted to do something physical to kick off my action steps.

2. I wanted to give myself the peace of mind that I could physically stand up for myself were I to face a situation where I could use some ass-kicking skills.

Therefore, during my amazingly productive strategy week, I called ahead and scheduled personal self-defense sessions at a local dojo.

I vividly remember the morning I had my first session. I wrote in my journal before, I wrote in it after, and even did a personal vlog. I created an angsty rock playlist I listened to on my walk there. I still felt so uncertain when I first walked into that strange new world by myself. But I realized within that first session with Master Tim that I was going to learn much more than just a couple moves. When it comes to self-defense, the aim is to exercise restraint, save your moves for when they're absolutely necessary, pay attention to your surroundings, and *don't be a victim.*

In fact, that was the priority: don't be a victim. That's a motto they share in self-defense classes nationwide, and what the hell! If it didn't fit into exactly what I was setting out to do and be! Don't be a victim—be an epic hero! You see, when you're building confidence in a physical form, it starts having this trickle-down effect through your mind and heart and soul. I've witnessed this in my role as a dance coach, but it had been so long since I had experienced the magic of initial discovery. The more I punched, kicked, and learned how to leverage the angles my small frame could make, the more I internally grinned at my new secret: I could take on anything that ever came my way.

That very first session, I started very timidly striking and kicking, but I grew bolder as the session progressed, and I started visualizing myself striking my negative thought patterns, not my teacher. I kicked down my self-doubt. I slugged my need for approval before making my own damn decisions. I sucker punched my false beliefs of limited capabilities. And I felt myself reclaim my confidence when I was taught and allowed to practice the "knee of vengeance" (or the knee to the groin). I called and texted my sisters that day to tell them I kicked a guy in the balls and how ridiculously freeing it was—I could hardly wait to share the empowerment I was experiencing through such a weird activity!

Now, there are many reasons people will find themselves using their fight chemicals, aka cortisol, for good other than just to blow up about getting the wrong french fry size at the drive-through. Many people turn that adrenaline rush into excitement and anticipation. Many people use those moments to protect others. My heart lifts when I see someone stand up to a bully for someone else. Even if one breaks into a physical altercation, there's something supremely noble about someone standing up for the defenseless or weak.

I personally encountered that type of hero the night before self-defense class, which I found very ironic and further enhanced my desire to know how to defend myself. I was on a train from the airport into the city very late that night when an unruly drunk passenger started causing a ruckus in my car. I tried to make myself very small, scooting far into the cold metal corner of my seat and situating my roller bag as a wall of protection in front of me. Somehow, that unruly passenger zeroed in on me specifically. He talked to me and tried to play music for me. I politely nodded and looked out the window, but he was determined to get my attention. He lurched into the seat next to me, pressing me even further into the corner, concerning me greatly that he might pass out or throw up right then and there, when another passenger, a tall, silver-haired man, physically pulled the drunk man up and away from me, saying, "No, sir, you cannot harass that woman." This upset the drunk man to the point that the train's security had to get involved, and it turned out to be a pretty dramatic ride. I never got a chance to thank that older gentleman who stepped in, but I truly appreciate his heroic actions that evening.

While I don't condone violence, I do have to admit that I loved taking self-defense and kempo, especially directly after that strange train ride. If you have yet to try out some form of martial arts, now is the perfect time to test it out! It is vastly empowering, and it seems to be normal for students to begin their training at any age. We are thrown such terrifying content in our faces every day that it's easy to feel overwhelmed with the fear of what's out there. But with just the knowledge that you have some raw ability to take care of yourself when push comes to shove (literally), it is a *huge* weight off your shoulders.

So now, let's set a goal: identify one thought pattern you would like to combat. Let's break it down and make it specific. It could be "I'm a terrible communicator," or "I can't make any friends because I'm so lame," or "I make the worst eating decisions ever." Next stage: let's fight it out! Whether you join an actual kickboxing class or you use a pillow, jab or kick with the opposite thought. Like "*I am awesome* at communicating!" Or "I can make friends with *anyone*!" Or "I make *excellent* choices with my diet!" Try it once, and if you don't feel the statement you chose is powerful enough, restructure and try it again!

I know that when you're in a relationship cleanse or recovering from any toxic circumstance, sometimes waking up and getting out of bed is a battle itself. So this is your permission to wake up and fight. You have to fight for freedom from the looming angst that traps you in your dark chasm. Fight the disparaging thoughts. Fight for your right to party. And fight your internal foe, coming out the other side victorious as your very own hero.

* * *

RECAP:

Journal time (or internal musing time)!

If we're combating victimhood, we're getting out of flight mode. Has there been a moment that stands out to you as being a missed opportunity to fight or stand up for yourself or others?

What stood in your way?

Which negative belief are you going to focus on fighting this week?

What physical action are you inspired to do to represent your kick-assery? (a special type of workout, kung fu, a dance battle, etc.)

Week 3:
Facing Fears

Life guru and mega mindster Mary Morrissey once described fear as the boundary of what you know.

How many times have you seized up before a new experience, a new roller coaster, or a new opportunity, palms sweaty, knees shaking, the questions of what will happen swirling around in your mind like a whirling dervish? And then, once whatever's causing that stress occurs, you almost laugh at how easy it was. I mean, that's not to say there aren't times when you actually feel like you've been hit by a Mack truck after such an occasion as well, but, surprisingly, that seems to be the minority of the time.

I love the concept of fear being a boundary. It makes it so much more palatable. But I have come to find that, apparently, my life is full of those boundaries because it's a pretty good day when I don't bump against a boundary or two, bruising my shin in the process. I'm definitely prone to mysterious bruises, but I'm sure it's just those damn boundaries I keep accidentally kicking. Some days I feel as though my knowledge-boundaries encase me in a pinball machine and I'm constantly bouncing from bumper to bumper until I finally fall down into the chasm between the flippers. Thankfully, I don't feel that way as much as I did once. Only occasionally.

Fear is fascinating to watch when in development. You can see toddlers fearlessly clamber all over furniture, falling, crying, only to get back up and do it again and again because they are curious and have flexible boundaries as they're learning about the world around them. Eventually, they piece it together and begin to realize, "Oooooh, every time I climb up onto the table from my chair, I fall off, and that never feels good, so I should probably explore another avenue of adventure." And eventually they realize the people around them, constantly warning that they're going to get hurt, were right. So they begin adopting fears from others because their experience has told them it saves them from injury, discomfort, and pain.

Once we realize there are laws of physics we can't really fight and that people throwing warning signs all around are often right, we start creating walls. We understand it serves us to play by the rules, and we fear breaking the rules because we want to avoid pain. We understand we could get hurt running around, so we start walking cautiously. We understand that some people are mean, so we decide to block people out until they prove us wrong. We understand that money runs out, so we live by strict and severe budgets and don't truly let ourselves enjoy our money and, essentially, our life as we're living it. I mean, screw that tropical vacation we've always wanted to go on! We will lose money if we go, and, additionally, we understand that sharks residing in tropical waters can be very dangerous, so boom! Two birds, one stone: no vacation and no sharks!

While these fears limit us a little, they are typically based on fairly reasonable rules. We keep safe in the midst of these boundaries, so we accept them as gospel. However, the issue with fears is that they keep us small. They often confine us to places we don't want to be. And fear is an ongoing victim's vice. Most everyone sympathizes with fear that stems from bad personal experiences, so it's easy for someone not yet shed of their victim mentality to commonly use "I'm afraid to trust anyone" and "I'm afraid I just can't trust myself" as excuses to keep from moving on and forward. And who can really argue with that?

Fear kept me in a toxic relationship for years. It was easy to push away the desire of changing things to pursue a life I really wanted when I was afraid of how my partner would react. I knew how to deal with my everyday fear of his everyday temper. It was almost like a companion to me in some strange way. It validated me being frozen in place, not really making decisions to get out of there. And I think this is quite common.

So if we're trying to push beyond that boundary, how do we do it? How do we fight fear? How do we conquer and vanquish it?

And you know what? You kinda don't. And by not doing it, you weirdly do.

Allow me to elaborate: Frodo didn't go to Mordor fearlessly, flipping the bird at Sauron, saying, "Here's what I think of your stupid ring, asshole!" He went *in spite* of his fear. The whole fellowship did! In fact, the job they did would hardly seem as heroic if they weren't all at least a little scared. But they were, and rightfully so, and they did what they had to do anyway. And that's a common thing in any epic hero's saga: there are always obstacles to climb that are terrifying, but a hero presses through the pain and discomfort of fear to achieve mighty things! So see? Fear is a boundary indeed! They say rules are made to be broken; I believe our boundaries are made to be shattered.

So today, think about what you're afraid of. Big or small, significant or funny, think about the things that give you the heebie-jeebies or make your palms sweat when you are in close proximity. Is it heights? Death? Public speaking? Clowns? The canned biscuits that you have to hit on the counter to open and that seemingly pop out of your hands with an explosion akin to that of a hand grenade? (Raising my hand here!) Okay, now let's home in on one of them and put on our fear lens. What is the boundary of knowing that is causing this to be a fear? For instance, with clowns, is it because you can't see someone's face and therefore their intention seems masked? If it's the canned biscuits, is it because it's just plain terrifying that pastry dough seems to come to life and it feels like you have a poltergeist terrorizing you every time you have to prepare them? (Thank *God* there are frozen options nowadays!)

Once we put the fear under the microscope, we can often see a more logical side to it accompanying our emotions, which is great because that's going to help us with our action step during this week. But it also unveils a more human, vulnerable need that might be a secret desire.

So let's say I decide to blast down a fear such as singing in front of people. And let's say I go to karaoke night and say, "Damn you, fear! I'm going to slaaaay a Whitney song with all the long notes and all the passion the late Ms. Houston gave in her greatest performance!" How do you think that will go? No practice, no thought, just go up and do it? Well, ripping the bandage off only helps so much. That might work, actually, for many instances. But let's say I entered that scenario, fear lens on. I know my fear stems from that one time in third grade I had a solo in the school play and forgot the words and choked in front of all my peers and teachers. So that's the boundary I know: in my experience, when I sing in front of people, I mess up and I feel like people judge me. So now that I see through that lens, let's say I wanted to confront that fear and be kind to it because I know it's based on a very human need to be accepted. Maybe I would walk into karaoke night, get to the front, and request a fun song everyone can sing along to like "Build Me Up Buttercup." Don't you think I would expand my horizon and boundary with that choice? Many people call it befriending your fear.

I now like to think of my fear as being a cute, giant mascot-sized fuzzy character that acts like my worried friend. My cute, miserable, blue friend follows me around, chiding me for wearing shorts when I haven't shaved my legs in a couple days, telling me to turn down a girls' trip invite because it will cost money when I'm trying to save, freaking out over what this or that person said to me once upon a time. I have a name for it. I call it my anxiety monster. It's super cute, though, and I just pat it on the head and say, "There, there, it'll all be okay. I'm smart, and today is a good day, and there's nothing truly to worry about in this matter." Personifying my fear has made a *huge* difference in how I perceive those boundaries, and I have a vastly different perspective when it comes to facing my fears.

You know, before the Olympics when athletes are asked by reporters if they are nervous, every single one of them will say, "I'm just super excited." Training the mind to identify adrenaline as something that could be used positively is a skill they've had to develop. Which is awesome because that's what we're going to train to do ourselves. Regardless of whatever outcome may occur, you have the power to drastically stretch your boundary with the attitude you have in approaching this.

So in our journey to herodom, we must make an effort to find the thing that scares us most and face it, acknowledge it, recognize it as our worrisome Piglet-like friend, and hold its hand as we approach our new boundaries. But wait! Before you freak out and think *Surely that can't be all! Hello! A little help here,* you're right. That's not all.

Practice thirty seconds of deep breathing. Here, I'll help you start:

Slowly inhale...

One...

Two...

Three...

Four...

Hold at the top for one...

Two...

Three...

Four...

Slowly exhale one...

Two...

Three...

Four...

Repeat three times.

Then say to yourself, "I'm allowed to have fears without them controlling me," three times.

When you get a moment to pop open a video or audio meditation, search for meditations to help clear anxiety. This should take you through similar breathing exercises and soothing mantras.

And now let's go back to those fears you thought about earlier. Can you look at them with a more objective perspective once you've allowed your mind chatter to settle a little? They might still seem a little daunting, but maybe a little smaller. And now I challenge you to befriend one of them. Ask it for its real name. Ask what it does and how it serves you. And then hold its hand and do something to ease it up a little! For me at this stage, it was posting some of my piano music compositions online, which I had never done before and made me feel so weirdly naked. I realized I had been artistically expressing myself my whole adult life for an approval stamp rather than letting my passion guide me and letting people seeing that work in progress. For you, are you afraid of mess? Have you ever had a mud bath? Are you afraid of dogs? Have you ever met a puppy at a shelter? Be creative! This is a new journey, and you'll be surprised what type of doors start opening to you when you're showing up for the universe in unexpected ways. The universe will be like, "Oh, hey! I didn't think I'd find you here! Huh. Fancy that! Well, while you're here, putting yourself out there with this whole rock climbing shenanigan, there's this opportunity to go hiking in Colorado with this cool group of people you just met and, like, they totally seem like your people, so why don't you go and enjoy yourself?"

Trust me: when you show up as a serious player, the world gives you some serious game. And once you crack open the seal, you'll keep finding new ways and new opportunities to face your fear, stretch the boundaries of what you know, and engage your bravery muscle, which will make you feel quite splendidly heroic.

* * *

RECAP:

Let's reflect and journal!

During this phase, I posted my music online for people to listen to and judge me by, which isn't a big deal to many people, but it terrified me. What's one thing you could do this week to stretch the boundary of what you already do or know?

We all have fears some might deem "irrational." What's one of yours? What's the story behind it?

We've all had to conquer fears in our past to grow and get from phase to phase in life. What's a fear you're proud to have faced and come out the other side stronger? What lessons did you learn from that experience that you could use to build your confidence in the next fear you have to face?

Week 4:

Sacrifice and Compassion

In looking through all the heroic stories I admire most, I recognize the fact that most of the fighting, the brutal journey, the sometimes brutish nature that would arise in the heroes stemmed from a desire to help mankind in some way.

You hear about the heroes of 9/11, and you picture immediately the selflessness demonstrated by firefighters and police officers in New York City. You think about the people who led others out of meeting rooms and offices to safety downstairs, ushering, coaxing, sparing little time for themselves to escape. In fact, you rarely call someone heroic in real life unless they risk something pretty big and act selflessly in that regard.

That is why we will now turn our focus to the qualities of sacrifice and compassion, two very beautiful, rare qualities that shine bright when things are darkest in the world.

One of my very favorite books of all time features one of my very favorite heroes. Sydney Carton was a slovenly drunk in love with a woman well out of his league. And he knew it. He shared his feelings, also admitted he was not worthy of her, and let her know if there was anything she ever needed in her life or something someone she loved needed, he had her back.

One of the reasons I truly love this character is that he is so seemingly unworthy of compassion and love because he never gave any to himself, and yet I can't stop rooting for him the whole narrative through. And then (spoiler alert) within the final chapters of *A Tale of Two Cities,* he embraces his higher potential when the opportunity comes to serve the woman he loves by saving her husband. In fact, he goes so far as to trade places with him at the guillotine, disguising himself as the husband. As he reflects upon the impact of his actions and how he is glad his life serves some good purpose on the planet, he muses, "It is a far, far better thing I do than I have ever done. It is a far, far better rest I go to than I have ever known." Which, of course, destroyed me and my romantic high-school self. I bawled for days over Sydney Carton and his sacrifice, and to this day I am still in awe of the brilliant mind of Dickens for conjuring up a character so perfectly developed from beginning to end with final words so beautifully heartbreaking.

Although not every hero sacrifices their actual life in their world-saving/people-saving actions, there is something they trade in for the greater good: ego, time, an arm, risk of being ostracized, a freshly cleaned shirt, or perhaps a broken nail. But the point is they risk greatly for the greater good when it's not necessary, which is outstanding behavior for any human.

I think of people who give generously even if they aren't a Gates or a Winfrey or anywhere close to the same zip code. I think about the people who volunteer their time to causes in their community regardless of their time-constraining workweek. These actions can be great or small, but in order to fully activate our heroism, we will need to sacrifice a little of something to achieve our higher potential. It means getting uncomfortable, pushing through that fear boundary, and doing something extraordinary for the greater good.

One huge thing that often gets overlooked when we are visualizing our sacrificial heroes, superheroes, and kick-ass assassin heroes is compassion. So if sacrifice is action, physical and outward-facing, compassion is its internal, mental, and spiritual companion. And it's not the same as pity. Pity often means you consider yourself and another on different tiers of life—they are lower and you are higher. Pity is regarding others as less than you. Compassion, however, raises them up, even if they are circumstantially beneath you, to where you are. Compassion levels the playing field.

There's a little moment in the newer live-action version of *Cinderella*, featuring the gorgeous Cate Blanchett as the stepmother and Lily James as Ella, where Cinderella is rescued from the tower in which she is trapped and hidden away by her stepmother. The prince isn't happy about finding her in such a place, his captain isn't happy, and it isn't looking too good for the "steps" at this point. But as Cinderella is being escorted by the smitten prince out of the house, her own childhood home in which she had been a servant to her own family for years, she turns to her stepmother and, in a sweet, kind voice, says, "I forgive you."

That moment destroyed me. I was about to bawl *hard* then and there in the movie theater because *wow*. Just *wow*. It seems so powerful, almost *superhuman*, to show compassion to someone who's been a real ass. And that brings us to forgiveness, compassion's healing, restorative BFF.

Let me be the first to say forgiveness is *super* difficult. I'm going to be real with you here—when I first did my superhero challenge, I didn't consider forgiveness to be a relevant course of action because my pain was so fresh and my ex was such an asshole. I was stubborn in my belief that there were just some things that were unforgivable. I knew wise sages like Gandhi, the Dalai Lama, and Jesus said otherwise, but what did they know of *my* circumstances and what I had been through? (Oh yeah, that's right: among Jesus's final words as he was dying on the cross were "Forgive them, Father, for they know not what they do." And that was about the people who had put him there!)

Because I initially avoided forgiveness, I left out a huge portion of super growth. I would encourage you to do otherwise. Now, let me be clear: forgiveness isn't where you insert yourself back into troublesome relationships to make sure everything's cool. That's not the point. You won't have to go have coffee with them, send them birthday cards, call them to chat as you wander around your kitchen looking for a late-night snack. No. Forgiveness is an internal process. If there is a circumstance where you feel it would be most healing to make amends, then by all means, do so, but don't think that's the same thing as buddying up to someone who might use you again once they feel it's all good between you.

Buddha once said, "Holding on to anger is like drinking a poison, expecting the other person to die," so think of forgiveness as being the antidote. And if you're anything like me back in my first bout of superhero-challenging, there are probably a lot of people you actively and/or secretly resent. So here's an exercise to help you identify where you need to start sending forgiveness vibes in your life.

First, think of your friends. Visualize their faces and pay attention to the feelings they incite. Is your energy positive? Do you feel lightness and humor and joy when you think of their faces? Great! Wish them well and move to the next group. Now visualize your work colleagues, especially the group you work closely with every day. If you work digitally and don't physically interact with them, just think of the virtual interactions between you. How do you feel about them? Think of each one. Do you feel lightness or neutrality? Or do you feel a tinge, a negative pull, when you think of the guy who always gets the last cup of coffee and doesn't bother to make a new pot for the people after him? And how about that person who seems to always make any virtual meeting about them and their soapbox?

Whenever you experience a negative feeling while thinking about a specific person, chances are that you probably need to let go of some resentment and begin a process of forgiving them. When you mentally come across that person, start repeating, either out loud or in your mind, "I wish you well." And as you repeat it, start smiling. Not a maniacal smile, but a genuine, friendly smile. It might feel funny and a little corny at first, but keep trying! We're doing some healing here, and if you've ever applied antiseptic to a wound, you know it feels funny at first as it's disinfecting, but then the wound is cleansed and can heal.

After your work colleagues, think of your family. This one can be quite intense for many people because of the long years of history with family that are filled with what Mary Morrissey likes to call "unskilled cries for love." But spend some time thinking of your siblings, of your parents, your aunts and uncles. Even if they've passed on, it's still very effective to think about them and untangle the harsh cords of resentment if they exist.

This exercise is the one I choose to do within my "shower thoughts" because I find that as I'm physically getting all cleaned off, it's a coordinating practice to cleanse my feelings of bitterness. And yes, it's a practice, not just a thing to do one time and announce, "I've fixed it all! All has been forgiven!" I still find cords of resentment I untangle a little more every day, and I am so happy and humbled that I have the perspective to release myself from that pain a tad more in my daily practices.

And now here's the most difficult of our forgiveness tasks: we have to forgive *ourselves.* The things others do that strike a chord in your heart strike hard for a reason—because it's a reflection of something within yourself that you don't like. It irks us to see it on someone else because it subconsciously reminds us of our insecurities or faults. We come across the reflection like a funhouse mirror and think it's another person, and they're looking at us funny and they're lurking and—*ow*! They must have just put their leg out to trip us and, oh no! Wait! We really just tripped over a loose board and, wait! There's no other person in the whole house—it's just you.

Forgiving oneself is a difficult task that must be a practice. Meditating, using positive mantras, and allowing yourself to treat yourself with kindness in moments of frustration are all ways that allow that thick, tangled knot of a thousand discords to loosen and be undone little by little. Forgiving yourself is like saving yourself, which is what we're attempting to do through this whole journey. So if you are to achieve one thing from all of this, I hope you take compassion with you for yourself and others.

When you're living in a compassionate, forgiving state, it's easy to sacrifice ego regularly, which is, by the way, essential for growth. And we want to become the highest potential, most kick-ass version of ourselves, don't we? So let's go forward on our hero's journey, sacrificing ego, sacrificing time and attention to our electronic devices to practice forgiveness and compassion. The world will thank you for it in many ways.

* * *

RECAP:

Journal and reflection time!

During this phase, I sacrificed my coffee addiction, I sought opportunities to donate food and clothes, I volunteered for tasks and causes outside my regularly scheduled programs, and I also recognized community heroes by taking a thank you card and box of treats to the local fire station.

What is something small you could give this week to exhibit the quality of sacrifice?

What could you do to sacrifice a bit of time that would help your community, friends, and family?

Sacrificing ego is a difficult practice at first, but we can start by showing compassion and forgiveness for those who have wronged us. Who can you start forgiving in your heart? And what in them do you see in yourself that you would do well to forgive yourself for?

Week 5: Battle Cry

Once upon a time, there was a monarch in England who had a stutter. Imagine what stress it must have been to be a member of the royal family and have a speech impediment! This monarch sought the help of speech therapist Lionel Logue, and the two began a very unorthodox student-teacher/king-subject friendship that allowed this king, or soon to be king, to feel truly heard as a person for the first time in his life. Logue helped him learn how to calm his mind to speak clearly, prepare for his coronation speech, and, essentially, believe in himself to take on the role as king of England. There would be years and years ahead of speaking to his kingdom and, in many cases, the world. Radio was growing increasingly popular during that time, and, oh yeah, there was a war brewing in Europe as well, so imagine the hope this man had to give his country in such a trying time! It was like a David and Goliath scenario—King George VI being David and his stutter, Goliath.

The film depiction of this story won the Academy Award for Best Picture that year, and it deserved it—that movie feels *so good* to watch! There is always satisfaction watching formulaic character growth in a story, especially in a public figure with an ongoing struggle having to constantly work at whatever elephant-in-the-room issue it may be while still handling the present business and matters in front of many eyes and critics is admirable and damn brave. I love to see that version of growth. Because it was hard—he worked, seemed to take two steps back from progress at times, but pressed on with the encouragement of his speech therapist and loving wife.

Every time I watch that movie, I feel a little bit seen. No, I am not part of the monarchy in any way. I'm not even on a single council. And no, I don't have the same level of struggle to speak. But my entire life I have found it difficult to speak up, tell people what I really want and believe, and I have been criticized for my hesitancy to communicate.

Growing up, I was the second oldest of six kids, which meant my main role was to help the younger siblings. I learned to not ask for help because there were younger children who needed help more than I did. I learned that when I voiced a desire, I was often answered with a good ol' "Do you think money grows on trees, honey?" Even when it came to buying new clothes, I felt criticized when I voiced my opinion on my fashions of choice and typically stuck to the sale racks at a supermarket supercenter. Looking back, I realize a lot of that was just my parents being parents, but I also recognize that my role in the family—not the oldest, not the bossy one, but more of the helper—placed me into a mentality that I continuously battle, that my voice didn't matter.

I have had many conversations with people who found themselves in abusive relationships, and I found that a similar mentality was extremely common in them: overly obliging, constantly putting others' needs first before theirs to the detriment of their own fulfillment, shutting up to keep the peace, and so on. We were given voices and perspectives the day we were born, but somehow, between then and now, we have gotten the idea that our voice wasn't really supposed to be used, it's bad when we use it, and to just lose it.

I *hate* that feeling. Like Bertie (or King George VI, rather), I found myself in many moments of life with the ability to communicate clearly only when all of my pent-up frustration burst out in a rage. I could plot out a civil conversation all I wanted, but when I came to the moment of actually having it, I'd stutter around, dodge points, pick at my cuticles, and couldn't seem to get the words out unless the conversation went south, and then I'd shout, "WHAT THE HELL DO YOU WANT ME TO DO?" And because I'm also a crier, I'd erupt and then feel bad that I couldn't clearly communicate, feeling doomed to never be taken seriously and start bawling (#adultingishard).

So my battle cry week was *extremely* important to me. I needed a full week to use my voice and tell people what I was doing, state my intention, and tell the universe what I wanted from this whole challenge. After looking at all of my heroes and their amazing qualities that I wanted to adopt as my own, I could see clearly I was going to have to develop a strong voice that could call to action my community and inspire people to help me change the world for the better. I think of every sports flick with the locker room "let's go out and play ball!" speech that turns the game around and leads to victory. I think about William Wallace's speech before charging into battle with the English: "But they'll never take our freedom!"

With the passion and energy connected with words full of intent and full of heart, great change occurs. I once had the privilege to see this type of empowering oration at a one-day Tony Robbins conference. If you have never seen him speak, he is a remarkable, true superhuman! His delivery on belief in the power of the individual who finds fulfillment is one of the most magical talks to behold. In person, his energy, even from hundreds of feet away, is palpable. When I watched him on stage pouring his passion out upon the arena, he looked like a great warrior, amping his army up for battle. I felt personally armed with incredible belief and grit—like I could conquer the world after even just a short afternoon listening to him!

Battle cry week was perfectly timed to kick off the second half of the challenge because from that point forward, my challenges would require communication and teamwork. Therefore I needed to build the belief that I was worthy to be listened to, that my points were valuable, that I had what it takes to inspire an army and nation (or community, or friend group, or whatever) and tackle the great hurdles my old foe, my victimhood mentality, would throw at me.

I had spent too much time believing I couldn't communicate, too many moments when I passed by a crucial conversation and suffered from the lack of voiced intent. It was now time to find my voice and know it was worthy of being heard.

So this is our focus: finding and using our voice. Letting it be heard above the din of busyness. Letting it herald and announce what you are intending with your life. Every great hero finds their voice and uses it to inspire people to build a better world, so that's what our intent is now.

Let's start by thinking about our personal mission statements. Start with why you are on this journey out of your victimhood.

Next, think about why it will help your community, family, and world for you to pursue this type of growth.

Next, think about what amazing things will happen in your life when you save yourself from victimhood.

And last, imagine what would happen if you *didn't* complete your transition to herodom. What do you have to lose? What will stay the same? See, we're going to use our worrisome friend, fear, a little for this one but in a good way.

Good. Now we've confidently stated to ourselves why this is important to us and what it means to us to fulfill our goal. Now let's include some friends in our journey.

Have you posted about any of your hero's journey on social media yet? That's a fairly quick and easy way to start, but let's take it a step further. Let's look a little ahead. Our next theme is "Adventure," and the following theme is "Superteam." If you haven't done anything yet to set up activities or get together with friends in our strategy stage, let's start reaching out! Invite people to go rock climbing, bike the city, explore a museum, masterfully escape an escape room, play paintball, ride horses, and hike the trails with you! Those would be excellent adventures for your next stage! Tell them why you will be doing it personally and then why it would mean so much if they joined you.

This was about the time I started confirming people for an activity I had planned for superteam week as well, letting them know how stoked I was that they were in my superteam and that I couldn't wait to celebrate that with them. Trust me: people like to feel like they're special to you and add to your life in a mighty way, so their being included in what you call a superteam, in my experience, makes people feel empowered to be your friend!

If you want to take using your voice a step further, start a blog and actually announce that you started a blog about your hero's journey and invite people to read it! Or a vlog! Overall, what we're doing is getting used to telling people our intentions and journey in a very empowered, positive way that is not intrusive to them but *inspiring* to them. Which brings up my final point.

Use your voice to lift people up. During this stage, text or call your friends and family. Try one a day, and give them some encouragement! Tell them what you think is awesome about them, a memory you have of them that brings you joy anytime you think about it, or just let them know that they make you feel valued and how much you appreciate that during this time of growth.

When emerging from the shadows of the chasm of victimhood, give out a mighty cry and rush forth toward the opening. Maybe others are trapped in there with you that you hadn't noticed before, and your voice is a call to action to follow you out! Maybe you'll find some exceptional companions and sidekicks to join you. Maybe you'll have some company as you journey into the *adventure ahead of you*…which, by the way, awaits you *next*…

* * *

RECAP:

Let's write down our intentions and let ourselves be heard!

This was the week I started a blog about my challenge, I became more vocal about what I was up to on social media, I wrote positive online reviews to help support local businesses, and I reached out to tell people what an awesome summer I was having because of the challenge and how they could be a part of it.

To help you get started being clear and confident with announcing your progress of this journey to your friends and family and the rest of the world, let's write down your mission statements.

Why is it important that you're doing the Eight-Week Superhero Challenge?

Why will it help your world/community/family for you to pursue this type of growth?

What amazing things will happen in your life when you save yourself from victimhood?

What would you have to lose if you didn't complete your transition to herodom?

What are two ways you can use your voice for good this week, whether for yourself or for others?

Week 6: Adventure

Every time I walk around a home decor store, I inevitably come across those little wall hangings that people put up around their kitchens and bathrooms and hallways, saying something along the lines of Adventure Awaits. It's funny to see such a casual reminder that adventure speaks to us all, especially on an object that will live in a pretty mundane space. But even the word "adventure" strikes an urgent chord in my heart within the walls of the home decor store.

There's a pulling of our hearts toward adventure, which is apparent when you look at the biggest blockbusters and best-selling novels of all time. We all have a thirst for adventure and the stories that narrate adventurous lives. It's in our curious nature. It's a suspenseful yet satisfying road to a goal—the more difficult the road, the more satisfying the victorious result.

And yet isn't it strange that adventure, although calling to all of us, rarely gets pursued by us? This is, of course, not including the occasional thrill-seeking roller coaster ride. But we would rather watch it on a screen and live vicariously through the characters embarking on their noble quests than dare pursue quenching the thirst ourselves.

Adventure, by definition, is an exciting and unusual experience or activity. It's extraordinary. And who doesn't want to live an extraordinary life? And by your terms, not anyone else's? We are already set up to live adventurously in that we all live unique lives. So we already have the "unusual" part of the equation. Now all we need is the excitement and enthusiasm and to engage in an activity!

I once had a friend go through a tumultuous marriage. She hid it well and kept smiling big and strong, but her health started failing rapidly for seemingly no reason, and she became difficult to even contact. It freaked me out a little that such a good friend seemed to be disappearing in every sense of the meaning. One summer we spent every Sunday by her pool drinking hard lemonades, and the next, I heard nothing from her or about her. It wasn't until I saw her at a conference that I was able to quickly catch up with her. Our chat was very brief and basically consisted of her informing me: "Sorry for not calling. My kidneys were failing. My doctors didn't know what to do. And my husband was being overly controlling and checking my phone, so I didn't feel comfortable calling you and being real. I'm getting a divorce. Gotta go."

I was speechless. My beautiful, bubbly, silly, empathetic friend was in so much pain, and I had no idea. We now lived states away from each other, so it was months before we were able to connect again and I could get a better idea of what was going on and how she was doing. And wow, those five months later, she looked so much better in every sense of the word! Her skin was rosy, her eyes were sparkling, her laugh was positively infectious again. It turns out she had embarked on a path of energy healing, going to a shaman and being taken through a spirit journey where she found her freaking golden spirit animal. She had gone to weekend trainings, immersing herself in intensive meditations and cleansing. All of these things brought her so much peace in her life post-marriage that she now offers healing services like that herself! Her adventure started internally for her health, but then she sought healers and groups of people to connect with externally to help guide her on her adventure, her journey, to heal from the inside out.

I have seen this many times with friends and acquaintances. After a breakup, they go to find a facet of themselves that develops strength, insight, and power in new experiences, countries, communities. They find themselves in *adventure,* each one a little different than the other.

Adventure is subjective. Raising a family is an adventure. Bungee jumping in New Zealand is an adventure. Training for a triathlon is an adventure. Getting that chic new pixie cut is an adventure. I had a friend once comment on my hair and ask what was going on in my life. I was startled by the comment because, well, *lots* of stuff was going on and how the hell did he know that? He chuckled and said, "Your hair's different. When a girl changes her hair, she's changing her life."

The point is adventure calls to each one of us differently. The question is, whatever the suggestion adventure has, do we answer it? Or do we shrug it off?

If you are feeling yourself slowly yet surely reaching the mouth of the cavern of victimhood, seeing the light ahead, and feeling the rush of hope in your heart, you might feel a surge of inspiration. Listen to it. When you're beyond a certain point of the chasm, you won't hear the echoes of depression as loudly anymore, and you'll begin homing in on a different voice. That voice has always been there, but it speaks calmly and quietly. And now that you're emerging to a calmer space in your mind, listen. Your intuition is chiming in. It's encouraging you to grow and do new things, chart new courses, discover a new life past the pain.

The difficult thing about adventure is that sometimes it can lead us into strange circumstances. It might have been the very thing that led us into that relationship with that unpredictable but ever so charming individual who ended up being a total shit show. And that's why it is so important to get to that calm place, that place devoid of echoes from your bleak past, that place on the cusp of hope, before setting off on that adventure. That way, your intuition leads you in a positive direction versus jetting off with that stranger from the bar, getting matching tattoos, and waking up in a hut in the Andes Mountains with no recollection of how you got there. (However, if you would like to write that book, I'd totally read it...)

When I embarked on my adventure phase, I was working out in California for a week, and coincidentally one of my very bestest friends in the world lived out in Los Angeles at that time. We were the kids in high school who wrote songs about cringe moments, who would hike up waterfalls, create new holidays together like "Utopia Day" (the first day of spring break), and plan our own surprise birthday party. So when it just so happened that my schedule landed me out her way during my adventure phase, *boom*. It was magic. All I had to do was call her and say, "Hey, Emily, I'm coming to California in July, and I want to have an adventure day with you! You pick whatever is adventurous in LA—I'm with you one hundred and ten percent, whatever it is!"

And, dear friends, when Emily is put to the task, she does not disappoint. The whole day was charming; it was an exploration of various nooks and crannies around LA, but the highlight was the double feature escape room. Talk about flexing your hustle muscle—that really hit the spot! Honestly, being locked in a room and given a timer and goal and puzzles really amped me up in all the best ways. I felt very satisfied that my Adventure Day with Emily was a hit!

Now, every engaging hero's story has an adventure in its storyline. Think through the heroes on your list, and I'm pretty certain there's not one who doesn't go through *something new* and *unusual,* some type of *journey* to fulfill personal *growth* and accomplish something *important* to them. And we can do this for ourselves! We can show ourselves that we are not only compassionate, communicative, and brave fighters and strategists, but we are adventurers capable of discovering new facets of ourselves through new experiences and opportunities.

My adventure challenge to you is this: try something new every day for the next five days. Whether by yourself or with your own "Emily," go out and find something interesting and experience it. Allow yourself to take a different route to work, try a new coffee shop, invite the new guy at work to lunch, climb a waterfall, wear a color you don't normally wear, go axe throwing…the possibilities are limitless!

Every day this week, wake up and think to yourself, *I'm going on a remarkable adventure!* Repeat it. Say it with gusto to your reflection. Say it to your goldfish, Frank. And actually *do it.* This is a very, very action-based phase, so stretch outside your normal routine and get creative. Yes, life is already an adventure in and of itself, but we can't see the grandness and the level of epic it has unless we truly and engagingly open ourselves up to discovering and experiencing new, unexplored territories in our lives!

Could you imagine what would happen if you, your friends, your family, and your community woke up every day with excitement and enthusiasm to face the unique day ahead of you? If you were flexible to possibilities that presented themselves throughout the day? If you greeted each person you met as a fellow adventurer? I wonder what would happen if we all didn't just hang the Adventure Awaits signs around our homes, and if adventure didn't have to wait around for us, kicking at the ground, twiddling its thumbs, calling out to us, "Hey, buddy, are you ready yet? Can you come out and play now?" I wonder what would happen if we chased it, played tag with it, grabbed it by the hand to dance with it, and pursued it daily in some way or another.

I've heard it said that we get to experiment with life, and I love that idea! I think I'll do just that by sprinkling in a little adventure wherever I can...

* * *

RECAP:

Let's get amped about our adventurous life!

During this phase, I let myself be taken in the current of adventure created by my friend for a day, but I didn't stop there! Every day, I tried a new food or drink. I said yes to all experiences that were presented to me. (I was very glad that I was surrounded by good friends most of the week to prevent me from getting into that waking up in the Andes Mountains with no recollection of going there scenario…)

What sounds adventurous and intriguing to you?

What's a new, small thing you could try today?

What's something fun and adventurous you could try this week?

Who's someone who could help you find adventure this week?

Week 7:
Superteam

You know that saying "Teamwork makes the dream work"? It's another one of those corny sayings you might find on framed motivational posters seen around the office or by the water cooler. Usually, when said out loud, it's followed by a high five or "Bring it in, team!" It's catchy, uniting, and effective because it's so true!

Notice how the word used in that chant is "dream." Not goal, not achievement. *Dream*. And I know—it rhymes with "team." It's great that it rhymes with "team" because in order to accomplish something beyond your current capability, which is what a dream is by the way, you must use means outside yourself. Our greatest resource in growing beyond ourselves is going beyond ourselves and learning from others. This is why the collection of your superteam, the community of people who make you feel strongest and most supported, is extremely vital at this stage in the game. You're tasting little moments of success and enlightenment by this point, but old habits die hard, and new ones might still feel like visitors unless we use our fantastic friends to help keep us accountable to our new self.

When I was in the midst of my hero's journey, I came to deeply appreciate the magic of my friends. I had some that lit me up. I had some that felt calming and restorative. And then I had people in my group that I noticed had different effects on me that I didn't necessarily want. I began pondering this, and since we were in the middle of a nice, toasty summer, I created this analogy.

Some people in your life connect to you like fireflies. You see them and sparkle a little to say "Hi!" They see you, and they sparkle back to say "Hi!" And then you swarm toward each other in this glowy, twinkling energy that lights up the room like a disco, and it's suddenly a party. I call my friend Stephen my fellow firefly because this is what happens any time we're in the same room.

Some people in your life are like a cool drink of water from the hose. Do you remember playing hard in the sun as a kid, laughing, sweating, running, and tumbling around with whimsy? And do you remember how refreshing it was to grab the nearest garden hose and hold it to your mouth as your friend lugged away at the faucet handle? And do you remember the rush of cool, refreshing hydration that came over you instantly, so that you could resume your regularly scheduled program of playing freeze tag for the zillionth time that afternoon? That's my friend Danyelle. She calms me down, cools me down, helps me get perspective and regain my social energy.

There are, I believe, opposites of those things, too, where you might believe someone's a firefly because they light up, but really they're a bug zapper and shoot you down. Or there are the people who seem like a cool drink of water from the hose, but they're really a dry well. But we won't worry about them too much now—you'll be drawing amazing vibes from people with the charismatic energy you're cultivating throughout this journey. Just be aware that some people may not be totally on board with you getting a life upgrade, and that's okay! There are plenty of other fireflies in the sky that think everything is exciting and awesome and plenty of cool drinks of water from the hose that think everything is interesting and cool.

Think through your close friends. You may have several, you may have one. As an adult, it can be a little challenging to find a large friend community, but you have some people on your side, no matter the amount. Do you have cool drinks of water from the hose? Do you have fireflies? Hopefully you can think of at least one of each type of personality connected to you somehow. If there are just a couple, that's great! Those are people with whom you can share your progress in your hero's journey and let them know what you intend on this path, and maybe they could do stuff with you to help you along the way! It's most advantageous if they have unique qualities from the others because your super squad needs diversity in its "superpowers."

And yes, we're creating a super squad for you because while you're on this journey, your overflow of joy, ambition, and empowerment needs to go somewhere it can be appreciated! And there is *power* when two or more people get behind a cause. When one starts lapsing into old thought patterns or habits, the other can cheer them on and help them back on the intended course!

Lately there has been a *plethora* of movies and TV shows where superheroes have joined forces with each other to truly save the world from an evil mastermind's world domination or destruction. Such a feat couldn't be done with just one of them, no matter how ridiculously indestructible they are. Nope. Not without the powers and support of the others, and that's how we're approaching this stage of our herodom. We need help in saving ourselves. I know—it sounds a little contradictory: to save yourself, you need the help of others to save yourself. But we've gotten to the stage now where we can trust ourselves a little more resolutely to find good people to join us.

When I was planning and getting ready for this week, I had checked in during my battle cry week on the invites to my birthday party, which I had planned to happen during this particular phase. Keeping in theme, I staged an unofficial superhero pub crawl, inviting my friends and colleagues and anyone who wanted to put on a costume and walk around Lakeview (in Chicago) all Saturday night that week.

I worked that Saturday and rushed home afterward to get ready. A friend of mine called and asked if he could get ready at my apartment since I lived across the street from the starting location. I said, Sure! Come on over! And I felt like a little kid playing dress-up as soon as he arrived. We had wigs and capes and accessories, and we were both in genderbending character costumes—I was Thor, complete with cape and hammer, and he was Edna Mode, complete with wig and glasses. I can't describe the amount of giggling that occurred as we finished the final touches and got to the front door. My friend, David, paused and remarked, "Oh my god, what if we're the only ones in costume?"

Well, I am delighted to inform you that we were *not.*

Every single attendee of my birthday pub crawl *wore a costume.*

And there were a good fifteen people who went from place to place in our group! The other patrons in the bars on our route would grow curious and ask, "What are you dressed up for?" To which my friends would exclaim, "It's her birthday!" while pointing at me as I posed with my hammer and cape. And the world opened up before us unlike anything I had ever experienced. We went to one bar, and the DJ and photographer there couldn't get enough of us. I felt like a party had been set up just for my super squad to enjoy. We went to another pub and enjoyed some games and music. Our final stop brought us to my favorite bar, where the owner allowed us to bust open a piñata a couple of my friends had brought with them.

Throughout the evening, in our walks from place to place, a question was tossed around: "What is your real-life superpower?" And I loved the responses, some of which turned into show-and-tell presentations. Hot hands. Makeup artistry. Durability. Useless trivia genius. Connecting people to each other.

That entire night is branded into my memory as one of the most hilariously fun nights I've ever experienced, and it originated out of a couple amazing things:

1. The 8-week hero challenge.

2. Daring to do something ridiculous but soooo cool to celebrate my birthday and my awesome friends.

Growth is sometimes painful and hard and tedious, but when you have friends to celebrate with, it reminds you how amazing life is, your growth is, and your *value* is.

So here is your mission, should you choose to accept:

In this phase, it becomes crucial to get people involved. One perfect way to get people excited about being involved in your mission is to celebrate them! I had a perfect opportunity to get my friends together since it was my birthday, but I know people would have been down with the whole thing had I applied the same energy and excitement to my invites, birthday or not! What's something you love to do? What's your idea of a fun time? What type of setting makes you feel free? Well, that seems like the perfect type of thing to do for some good ol' friendly QT, don't you think?

Now let's think about your friends. As much as it would be great to get them all together and have the time of your lives in the same place at the same time, maybe that's not everyone's style. In fact, I can guarantee it isn't. In that case, recognize what your friends respond to. What is their love language? How do they like to connect to you? How do they like people connecting to them? Sometimes those things are different! For instance, I have a friend who loves doing things for others but feels stressed when others go out of their way for him. Another friend loves one-on-one time, can't seem to get enough of it, but jets out of bigger gatherings early. Think of those things and connect with friends the best you can during this phase! Write them notes, send them surprises, take them to lunch, post a shout-out on social media, gather them together for game night, go to a comedy club and laugh until your sides ache, take lots of pictures, and let them know you've got their back just like you know they've got yours. All for one and one for all and all that, right?

And if you're really feelin' it, maybe you'll discover that friend who will help you in your next phase. The big one. The *jumbo* look-at-me-world, I-got-this-shit, cherry-on-the-tip-top-with-extra-sprinkles moment. If not, at least you have people waiting at the edge of their seats, popcorn in hand, eager to see what happens next...

* * *

RECAP:

Let's journal and reflect about our framily, shall we?

In this phase of my challenge, I invited my local friends to go on a superhero pub crawl, which turned out to be the most fun evening I had ever put together! And since I have friends all over the country, I used my social media platforms to give shout-outs all week to the people who have impacted my life immensely with their friendship and support. I've continued the practice of celebrating my friends with sending them occasional "just because" gifts and texts and organizing weekends, nights out, and virtual friends' nights with them.

Who are some people in your life you know have got your back no matter what? What superpowers do they possess?

What are three things you could do to celebrate them this week?

What's one thing you would like to do to continue celebrating them and demonstrating your gratitude for their friendships?

Week 8:
Learn to Fly!

And now, my friends, we have come to the final stage of our hero journey. This is the cherry on top, the grand finale, the North Star, the big *ta-daaaaa,* the final act in our epic saga, the climax!

You see, until this phase, you have been putting in the work. You have been setting forth with the intention of growth and progression. You started this journey from a darker place, and like a true storyline, you have had your ups and you have stumbled through downs (which is to be expected in chapters of growth and change). You've sacrificed, you've fought, you've gone on this very intentional journey, and therefore it is time for the big grand gesture to yourself.

This is the part where you create your own version of what "grand gesture" means. What would take this journey, sum it up, and stamp it with a memory that you would be hard-pressed to ever forget? I realized that at this stage of the game I needed to do something that would be the perfect ending to this eight-week journey so that I could always remember this challenge, this epic phase of life, and connect it with a feeling of solid accomplishment.

Back in strategy week, I had figured it out. Back when I was connecting with friends during the battle cry week, I found someone who wanted to go with me. So not very long after my epic superhero birthday party, my good friend Chris and I drove a couple hours outside of Chicago to this massive campus of thrill seekers and world travelers on an airstrip. As we pulled up in our rental car, beautiful colors filled the cloudless sky in tiny dots that grew larger and more vast as they descended. This was the first time I had ever been to a property full of skydiving enthusiasts, and it was a sight to behold!

As I got out of the car and walked toward the giant warehouse-sized facility to check in, I looked around and suddenly felt like the least cool person in a ten-mile radius. I didn't have dreadlocks. I had no tattoos. I had no extra facial piercings. I wasn't even wearing cargo pants. I realized I should have looked on the website a little more to see what would be most appropriate to wear for such an occasion, but I didn't. The joggers and workout top would have to do. So I shrugged, recognized my doubts were stemming from a deeper place of caution, hushed it down, and strode forward with feigned conviction.

When I realized I was starting to use the insecurity of what I was wearing, that I must look so lame and new, that maybe I was too tired to try something so adrenaline-inducing that day, I held on to the faith I had been building for the past seven weeks. This was going to be my big grand gesture, and no one, not even my worrisome anxiety monster, could talk me out of it. I got my registration papers and liability papers, and I signed my name loud and clear because I was going skydiving, dammit, and there wasn't a thing I could do to stop me!

And see, that's what I acquired through this journey: a collection of feelings and convictions that I can, indeed, do the things I want to do, even if they seem to be beyond the realms of the Dani I am in that moment. That I am, indeed, a person of strength and adventure. And now it was going to be tested in the coolest way I could possibly think of.

After all of the other fun activities, facing fears, fighting, gathering friends, I came to realize that this grand gesture was more than just another one of those things—it was the ultimate "post that shit!" moment summarizing it all. It was something that made me feel like I had to use the skills I had trained within myself all mushed into, literally, one giant leap.

I went through the pre-jump training, met my tandem jump instructor, hired a photographer to jump with us to capture the whole thing (which, by the way, is a *brilliant* investment if you really want some kick-ass images of how kick-ass you are). As my nerves were building, accelerating to speeds I'd rarely experienced in my adulthood, I reminded myself, *Shh, Dani. You've always wanted to do this. Remember: this is the dream! We've worked up to this! You've got this!* I am glad to say my positive inner chatter outspoke the negative "what ifs". My camera guy interviewed me before my jump for my skydive video, asking me how I was feeling. I don't remember this at all, but I have it on video, so I guess it actually happened where I completely and calmly responded to his posed questions with unbothered grace. It was weird seeing myself in my harnesses and gear saying, "I am very excited. It's something I've wanted to do for a long time, so I'm proud of myself for finally doing it."

Soon I found myself in a tiny, tightly packed, seatless airplane, my instructor strapped closely to my back. My photographer began taking pictures and videos of Chris and me, getting our final reminders of how to check the altimeter strapped on our wrists like watches and how to release the parachutes. I was nervously nodding and smiling, hardly hearing a word over the buzz of the engine and the air whooshing outside the plane. My mouth felt like it was full of cotton, and I couldn't remember the last time I had a sip to drink. We climbed higher and higher, my ears feeling more and more packed, needing to pop, my breath exercised more by reminder than by natural function.

I can hardly remember the details of the short flight, but I remember vividly the feelings swirling around and how I fixated on one: I was so excited about meeting the version of me on the other side of the jump. I was in the very back of the plane with my instructor and photographer. The doors opened ahead, and one by one people began tumbling out. It was all a blur because all I could think about was my transformation of self between the jump and the landing. That's what I focused on. I let it fill my mind, I let a smile dominate my expression, and I captured that moment in my heart.

I watched Chris drop out ahead of me with a big "Yahooooooo!" I grinned bigger and thought, *Me too! I can't wait to meet the version of me on the other side of this jump.*

Then I realized I was the last one left to jump. I looked out of the door, feeling like I was seeing the world's surface for the first time. Loose strands of hair escaped my ponytail and whipped around my face as I grinned at the photographer perched just outside of the plane door. This was such a real version of victory or death. And I was pretty sure I was going to come out of this victoriously (and with some pretty rad pictures to share).

The world was a patchwork quilt of greens and yellows, the hazy blue an ombré effect on the horizon. The hazy, great blue, my playground for the next eight minutes during my descent. It's funny how I've always looked at the sky in wonder yet had such little personal interaction with it. At least, until that moment. At that moment, I was about to pass a boundary I hadn't even realized existed—the boundary of where I existed in the world. Funny how it held such deep meaning in so many ways, this action. Funny how I had changed my perspective of the world in so many ways, and here I was truly understanding how big a perspective shift I had undergone. Funny how I was excited to fall twelve thousand feet to the earth with a stranger strapped to my back and a stranger falling beside me while snapping pictures at my flappy-skinned face.

As these thoughts collided and tumbled together like polishing stones, the overlying, most emphasized, bold-italic thought that superseded the rest was ***I can't wait to meet the version of me on the other side of this jump.***

And I fell.

This has become a mantra in my life. There are many big leaps to take, many planes to tumble from. This book, for instance, is a version of skydiving for me. But I now have full confidence that I can make it out on the other side and that the person I'll become on that side is worth the trouble, the pain, the fear that stands between me here and me there.

So when you come to this peak in your journey, think of it as your personal "TAAAA-DAAAA, look what I can do now!" moment. You have just dedicated yourself to healing through this Eight-Week Hero Challenge, so let's honor that in a giant, memorable way! Not every challenge can finish with a skydive. I recognize that won't always work. But I strongly believe in making the big grand gesture with that adrenaline and conviction of action and character.

My encouragement to you is to do the thing you've always wanted to do! If you feel your intuition screaming at you to tattoo your favorite quote somewhere that will remind you of your hero's journey, you have my blessing. If you feel so inclined to hike Machu Picchu, do it as soon as you possibly can! Or sing "Don't Stop Me Now" at live-band karaoke with backup dancers. I'm totally there in spirit, front and center, cheering and waving my arms like crazy! Basically, this last challenge is about seizing the day, the moment, and making it the minute you've always dreamed of living. You deserve it! You deserve to live victoriously, celebrating the growth you've achieved and the next chapter of life up ahead. Tell yourself, "I can't wait to meet the version of me on the other side of this!" And take that saying with you to chant in the gym, to your red, crying face in the mirror after a bad day, in hard-core study sessions, when deadlines are pressing. Because if you can save yourself from the grips of victimhood, you can do just about anything!

I landed on my feet after my jump. They had trained us to land sitting, but I got my footing easily, and I managed to have a smooth landing, my face beaming, my eyes teary. I felt joy bubbling up in laughter as Chris greeted me at the landing stretch with high fives. My camera guy brought up the rear of my welcoming committee to interview me post-jump. I felt like a freaking rock star. And the funny thing with all of my mantra-ing, my turning nervous energy into excited energy, and everything else is that the me I met on the other side, I was pleasantly delighted to discover, wasn't much different than the me on the plane, or the me in my superhero pub crawl dressed like girl Thor and traipsing around Lakeview, the me conquering two escape rooms within two hours with two friends, the me who made myself vulnerable in a posted video of my original piano composition, the me who took her first self-defense class and decided to pick up fighting as a new hobby in general. Nope—I wasn't too different. It was just like going up in the plane; I gained the perspective on how all the world, and now even the sky, was so accessible to me. I now had a new perspective of myself. I discovered parts of me that had gone unnoticed but have always been there. And I've always been kicking ass in one way or another.

Now I was just ready to accept it.

* * *

RECAP:

Grab your pen and journal—we've got some reflecting to do!

In this phase of the challenge, I let myself accomplish one big thing. After my skydive, I continued to observe myself and notice the big shifts of perspective that had occurred during my summer.

What would be a grand gesture to you? What could you do that would signify that you proudly claim your herodom and that you're shedding your victimhood?

In what ways have you generally felt braver from this journey?

I called this week my "Learn to Fly" phase, but that's symbolic of my action. What's an empowering title for your grand gesture week?

Who are you meeting on the other side of your TA-DAAA moment?

The Ongoing Hero's Journey

And now we've come to the end of this particular journey. I look back at my first run through the Eight-Week Hero Challenge with utmost fondness and gratitude as I took a giant leap in fulfillment of potential from that experience—the things I've learned, the things I've done, the people I've connected to, the person I've become…

When you have reached the close of this hero's journey, look back. What did you discover about yourself? What truths did you uncover? What lifts you up? What provokes you and threatens to bring you down? Are you brighter? Are you laughing more? Are you challenged more? Are you willing to fight for your right to party? What are you keeping with you into the next leg of your life's journey?

I found as I closed that chapter that it was only a preface of the ones following. A couple weeks after my challenge was finished, I found myself in a dive bar in Texas, rapping some old-school '90s hip-hop at karaoke night. It wasn't a great performance, but I had a blast and my friends seemed entertained. A few weeks after that, I reconnected with a dear friend from the past, and we danced the night away at Britney Night at a club in Boystown, Chicago. A couple weeks after that, I went skateboarding for the first time at sunset in the New Mexico desert. A couple weeks after that, I choreographed a lip-synch battle performed in Vegas. And a couple weeks after that, I started dating again.

You see, the challenge opened me up to saying yes to so many things and experiences that, no matter where I looked, doors were opening to me. The whole world was lighter, everywhere. I liked who I was seeing in the mirror for the first time in *ages.* And let me tell you what—people noticed. People reacted positively and enthusiastically to the changes I made. When you start embracing the beautiful, adventurous parts of you, the hero within, the world embraces you back.

So how do we maintain this beautiful sensation of positive, enlightened growth? How do we keep our life charmed and charged and prevent it from going back into its cursed rut?

First, continue to plan time for *you,* what you need, what you want, and what you would *love*! Create daily rituals that you make personally sacred. Create fun, giant goals that might scare you a little, and take baby steps to help make them accessible. Dream big and do one thing a day or week to try on your dream for size. You can do anything, so might as well try to do the things that make your heart sing!

Continue to fight. Whether that means you pursue a martial arts practice as a continuous reminder that you got your own back, or you start a petition to create change in your community, or you continue to stand up for yourself, what you want, and what benefits others around you, keep doing it. You've got the power!

You've got the strength! Practice it. Don't let it go. Fight for the ability to keep changing and being flexible; fight for the things you know to be true.

Continue to face your fears. Continue to make friends with them and push their boundaries. Show them compassion to show yourself compassion. Continue to embrace them, hold their hands, and let them join you on your ride without them dictating where that ride goes. Find ways to confront your fears on the regular, so that when the big ones come at you, you know you can win that standoff!

Continue to show compassion and give. Practice your forgiveness prayers, give to charities, volunteer at the local animal shelter, hug a friend in need. Let the world know through your actions that you're here to help make a positive difference—the world will thank you!

Continue to use your voice for good. Speak up, tell your truth, tell your friends and family that you love them, write positive online reviews, tell people what you intend so that you are accountable to fulfill your intention and so they know how to help you.

Continue to seek out adventure. Try new things, go to new places, meet new people. Discover parts of yourself in the moments of discovering new things. Live to the fullest ounce of vitality your body constantly shows up to give you.

Remember that it takes a village, that you have amazing people in your life that color your world brilliantly, and celebrate those amazing people, your tribe, your super squad. And let them celebrate you! Recognize that two heads are better than one and asking for help isn't weak—it takes lots of strength and confidence to ask people to assist you in accomplishing your dreams.

And remember to do the daring thing, the *big* thing, the thing that makes people say "Oh, they're not really going to do that, are they?!" Prove them wrong. Prove yourself right—that you have the nerve, the courage, the audacity to do the thing most people only ever dream of doing. And look forward to meeting that person on the other side of that great, big, grand gesture.

Now, remember, we are ever growing, but we are never built completely from scratch stage to stage, so there will be doubts, there will be old thought patterns, there will be treacherous mind chatter that will try to pull you down. The hero has emerged, but the villain is only in hiding, the victim waiting in the bank for the robbers to come busting in to hold them hostage. But after these phases of growth, after exemplifying these eight heroic qualities in yourself, you've proven that you are more than the average bear. So hold on to that. No matter what happens around you, whatever circumstance in which you find yourself, hold on to the fact that you have your superhero catsuit waiting just under your civilian clothing, and you have the power to combat anything ahead that gets in your way of living an extraordinary, amazing life! I don't know about you, but I want an extraordinary life. To have an extraordinary life would be the most self-loving thing to do.

When you know this about yourself, when you hold on to this belief, it isn't just a service to you and your mental health but to those around you. You become a light, a beacon of hope to those who might be trapped in their own personal chasms. You become an inspiration!

So what are you waiting for? Go live the life you want to live! Go serve the world in whatever way you want to serve it! And if ever you doubt who you are, look at what you've done and who you've become: you are a freaking hero, a *superhero* of a human, and the world is lucky you took the time to discover that.

* * *

RECAP:

First of all, wow. You read this entire guidebook to hero living, and that is amazing! I hope you feel like you just gave yourself one giant hug in the process.

I look back on this superhero challenge as being one of my very favorite chapters in life. I use it as reference when I feel my old doubts creeping into my mind. I show to my doubts the evidence of my capabilities and my kick-assery, and my doubts back down.

So what have you discovered about yourself in this journey?

Which phase did you find the most challenging?

In which phase did you feel yourself soar?

What are you hoping to take with you after this challenge?

Have you discovered a superpower you didn't realize you possessed?

What are you hoping to do now that you realize you're not a victim or villain but a freaking-awesome superhero?

About the Author

Dani Atkins is a professional ballroom dance coach/judge/competitor and a Certified Life Coach who has trained amateur and professional dancers from coast to coast. Dani strives to combine personal development along with the physical training she gives her students and clients on the dance floor.

Although this is Dani's debut book, she has been writing every day for the past twenty-five years in the form of blogs, training manuals, blurbs featured online and in magazine articles, and corny poems found in random coffee table books.

Currently residing in Grand Rapids, Michigan, Dani enjoys spending time golfing, baking, writing music, playing piano, exploring pretty much every avenue of curiosity that piques her interest, and spending time with her boyfriend and his kids.

www.ingramcontent.com/pod-product-compliance
Ingram Content Group UK Ltd.
Pitfield, Milton Keynes, MK11 3LW, UK
UKHW020416250726
13967UKWH00007B/2673

9 781685 150389